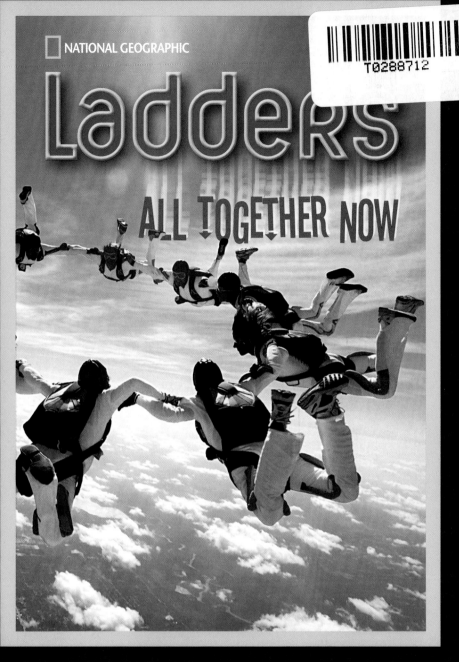

NATIONAL GEOGRAPHIC

Ladders

ALL TOGETHER NOW

Together

by Barbara Wood and Ken Novak | illustrated by Kevin Zimmer

Coordinate, collaborate,
That's what people do
Together in communities
Of folks like me and you.

Businesses coordinate
To put goods* on our shelves.
If they didn't work together
Could we do the job ourselves?

Construction crews* collaborate,
Build bridges, homes, and streets;
Restaurants collaborate:
They make us food to eat.

Neighborhoods cooperate
With libraries and schools.
Students, parents, teachers, too
Learn, play, and follow rules.

Departments called *Police* and *Fire*
Respond if you can phone.
Communities **accomplish** tasks
We cannot do alone!

*goods   things people buy and sell
*crews   groups of people who work closely together

Check In   What are some of the things people do in this poem?

3

The Argument

by Hilary Wagner
illustrated by Jim Bernardin

Chapter One

Viola slumped at her desk and rested her chin in her hand. She glanced at Abbey, Max, and Ling, her best friends, and they looked just as gloomy. Normally they'd be talking and laughing as they got ready for the bus, but not today. The day had started out so well. How had it ended so badly? What had even started their argument?

Viola got on the bus and thought about the day's events. It had all started when Miss Wallace announced that everyone would be doing skits about insects, which they had been studying. Viola was thrilled because she and her best friends had been put in the same group. They were supposed to do a skit about harvester ants and how an ant **colony** works.

Quickly putting their desks together that morning, the friends got to work.

"We could be ants in the colony," said Abbey, "and have different jobs."

"I can write our lines," offered Max.

"Whoever plays the queen ant should have the most lines," said Abbey.

"Who gets to be the queen ant?" asked Ling.

"I should be the queen," said Abbey, "since it was my idea."

"But I've been in the most plays," said Ling. "So I should be the queen."

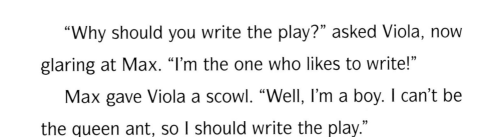

"Why should you write the play?" asked Viola, now glaring at Max. "I'm the one who likes to write!"

Max gave Viola a scowl. "Well, I'm a boy. I can't be the queen ant, so I should write the play."

"We can't help that you're a boy," said Abbey, folding her arms in a huff. She turned to Ling. "And why should you be the queen just because you've been in the most plays? That's not fair!"

"But I have the most experience," said Ling. "So I should have the biggest part."

"I think I should be the queen," said Abbey, "and you can make the props."

"I don't want to make the props," said Ling, folding her arms like Abbey had. "Besides, Max is the one who likes art."

"You want me to write the skit and make the props?" asked Max. "That's most of the work!"

"I don't want you to write the skit," said Viola. "I want to write the skit!"

The argument got worse. As the friends got louder, Miss Wallace came over and talked to them about the importance of **collaborating** with one another.

Collaboration, thought Viola, looking out the bus window. How was that even possible? She looked back at Abbey, Max, and Ling. They sat in silence, staring out their windows. How could they all get along if they weren't even speaking?

9

Chapter Two

Viola was still upset about yesterday's fight, but she woke up with a new outlook. Today her class was going on a field trip to an insect museum. This museum had all kinds of insects, from beetles to bees. It even had a real harvester ant farm! Miss Wallace said the ant farm was kept under glass. You could see the colony up close and watch the ants all working together to keep their community going.

Still not speaking, Viola, Abbey, Max, and Ling filed off the bus with the other students and walked into the museum. All of the other kids were smiling. They were excited about their visit. Viola wished she could get her friends to smile again. Miss Wallace organized everyone into their groups and sent them to find the display for their assigned insect. In awkward silence, the four friends stepped into the room that held the harvester ant farm display.

They couldn't help but gasp as they entered the room. The farm was huge, taking up almost an entire wall. It was made up of flat glass boxes all connected by thin tunnels, making a vast colony of ants—a swarming mini city. Viola and her friends stepped closer to the display, trying to get a better look. Thousands of tiny ants were all **coordinating** their roles like the parts of a well-oiled machine.

Max read one of the labels on the display. "Look," he whispered, "this is where they store their food, so they never go hungry."

Viola stepped closer and looked at the ants. One by one, they carried small crumbs on their backs and took turns placing them all together. "They must be the food gatherers," she said. She admired how well they worked, like teammates.

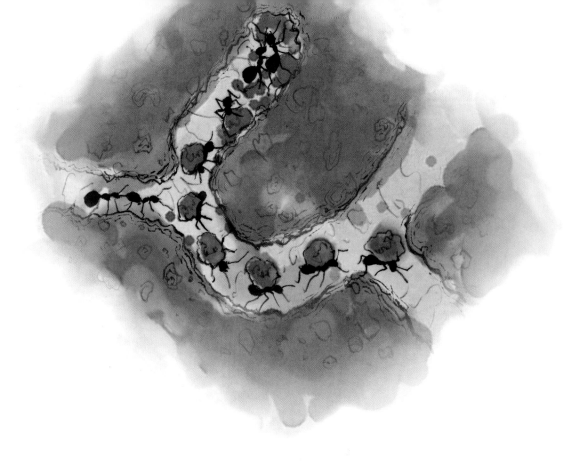

Ling waved the others over. "Look," she said, "this group of ants is making a new tunnel." The ants seemed to be adding onto their community. They were digging out a new passage. Each ant was collaborating with the other workers to remove pieces of soil.

"They're so patient," said Abbey.

"You'd have to be patient to build an entire city," added Max.

"I guess if you work together, you can **accomplish** just about anything," said Viola.

The four friends shared guilty glances.

Seeing the ants working together made Viola realize how silly yesterday's argument had been. Working as a team and putting on a great skit was more important than fighting over jobs. These ants worked together in order to stay alive. If ants could do that, surely she and her friends could do their skit without arguing. They wouldn't accomplish anything unless they worked together.

Viola realized she had been selfish. She smiled at Max. "I'm sorry I yelled at you about writing the skit. It's okay with me if you write it. You'll do a great job."

Max watched the ants dig out their tunnel. "I was thinking maybe you should write the lines. That way I can make our props. I like art more than writing anyway."

Viola smiled. "That sounds okay with me. But may I help you with the props?"

Max nodded. "It'll be a lot of work, so that would be great."

Abbey nudged Ling's shoulder with her own. "You can be the queen ant, if you want. I'd like to be one of the builders and show how the ants dig a tunnel. You're better at memorizing all the lines anyway."

Everyone worked as a team for the rest of the week. After Viola wrote the lines, Abbey checked the grammar and made copies to pass out. Viola helped Max paint their four ant masks in shiny shades of brown. Ling helped Abbey memorize her lines after school. After several rehearsals, the four friends finally felt they had it right. They each played a harvester ant coordinating its own job with the jobs of the other ants.

Chapter Three

The big day had arrived. Miss Wallace called their group up to the front of the class. Being the first group to perform, everyone was a little nervous.

"What if I forget a line?" whispered Abbey before they began.

"You'll do fine," said Ling, squeezing her hand. "You worked really hard in the rehearsals."

Viola looked at Max. "What if no one likes the skit?"

"Don't worry," said Max, helping Viola put on her ant mask. "You're the best writer in class."

Everyone clapped loudly. They loved the skit! Abbey didn't forget any lines, and Max's harvester ant masks impressed the whole class. Miss Wallace said they'd done an excellent job of showing how ants work together. As Viola turned in a copy of their skit to Miss Wallace, she thought of the harvester ant farm. She wondered if ants ever put on skits. If they did, she knew they'd do an excellent job, too.

Check In How did Viola and her friends help one another?

HELPING HANDS

by Renée Bauer

Owning a home is too expensive for many people. Sometimes families have to live in places that are unsafe or unhealthy. For example, these homes may not have water or heat. The neighborhood may be dangerous, too.

Meet Habitat for Humanity. This group's mission is to build **affordable** homes for people in need.

The women in pink hard hats are nurses. They came to help Habitat rebuild a community.

Millard and Linda Fuller started Habitat for Humanity in 1976. They believed everyone ought to own a good home. Today more than two million people live in a house built by Habitat's **volunteers.**

Habitat for Humanity supports families, communities, and even its volunteers. Families gain a good place to live, and communities become safer as more people own good homes. The volunteers get to develop new skills, be outdoors, and meet new friends. Therefore, Habitat for Humanity is a group that is good for everyone involved.

Families chosen by Habitat for Humanity must work hard. They must help build the house they will own. Habitat gives them an affordable loan to help pay for their house. Loan payments fund the building of more houses for other families. Habitat's homeowners can take pride in what they have **accomplished.**

Habitat's mission affects neighboring communities, too. Neighborhoods become more pleasant to live in. People may go to more community events once they own a home. They may try to prevent crime and keep their neighborhood clean.

Building a house may be hard work, but it is worth the effort. Volunteers learn useful skills. For example, they may learn how to use a drill or put up the frame of a house. They also learn how to **collaborate.** Since building a house takes so many steps, the volunteers must **coordinate** their work in order to build a house that will last. And, as everybody works together, they make new friends.

Volunteers work together to achieve a goal.

Habitat for Humanity benefits families, communities, and its volunteers. Habitat builds more than homes. It builds better lives, stronger communities, and lifelong friendships!

Check In   How does Habitat for Humanity help people in need?

23

Discuss Text Structure and Point of View

1. What do you think connects the three pieces that you read in this book? What makes you think that?

2. The poem "Together" has five stanzas. Describe how you think the first stanza is connected to all of the other stanzas.

3. In "The Argument," did you agree with one character's point of view more or less than with those of the other characters? Why or why not?

4. In "Helping Hands," what was the writer's opinion or point of view? Cite evidence from the text to support your answer.

5. What do you still wonder about any of the pieces in this book? What questions do you still have after reading?